Hurricane Opal in Florida

A BUILDING PERFORMANCE ASSESSMENT

August 30, 1996

FEDERAL EMERGENCY MANAGEMENT AGENCY
MITIGATION DIRECTORATE

The Building Performance Assessment Team Process

In response to hurricanes, floods, earthquakes, and other disasters, the Federal Emergency Management Agency (FEMA) often deploys Building Performance Assessment Teams (BPATs) to conduct field investigations at disaster sites. The members of a BPAT include representatives of public sector and private sector entities who are experts in specific technical fields such as structural and civil engineering, building design and construction, and building code development and enforcement. BPATs inspect disaster-induced damages incurred by residential and commercial buildings and other manmade structures; evaluate local design practices, construction methods and materials, building codes, and building inspection and code enforcement processes; and make recommendations regarding design, construction, and code issues. With the goal of reducing the damage caused by future disasters, the BPAT process is an important part of FEMA's hazard mitigation activities.

About the Cover

THIS PHOTOGRAPH WAS TAKEN ALONG THE GULF COAST IN THE CITY OF PENSACOLA BEACH, FLORIDA, AFTER THE PASSAGE OF HURRICANE OPAL. IN THE FOREGROUND ARE THE REMAINS OF A STRUCTURE BUILT BEFORE THE CITY ADOPTED THE FLOODPLAIN MANAGEMENT ORDINANCE REQUIRED FOR PARTICIPATION IN THE NATIONAL FLOOD INSURANCE PROGRAM (NFIP). THE STRUCTURE IN THE BACKGROUND WAS BUILT AFTER THE ADOPTION OF THE REQUIRED ORDINANCE AND WAS THEREFORE REQUIRED TO MEET NFIP STANDARDS FOR CONSTRUCTION IN THE COASTAL HIGH HAZARD AREA. THE DRAMATIC DIFFERENCE BETWEEN THE POST-STORM CONDITIONS OF THESE TWO STRUCTURES UNDERSCORES THE IMPORTANCE OF PROPER CONSTRUCTION IN COASTAL AREAS SUBJECT TO HURRICANES.

Table of Contents

Executive Summary

On October 4, 1995, Hurricane Opal made landfall on Santa Rosa Island, Florida, near Navarre Beach, at approximately 6:00 p.m. c.d.t. (central daylight time.) As a result of the damage caused by Hurricane Opal, President Clinton declared 15 counties in the Florida Panhandle and Lee County, on the southwest Florida coast, Federal disaster areas (see Figure 1-1).

The Federal Emergency Management Agency (FEMA) deployed a Building Performance Assessment Team (BPAT) whose mission was to evaluate structural damage and recommend mitigation measures that will enhance the performance of buildings in future storms. The team was composed of engineers and building construction specialists from FEMA, the State of Florida, and the private sector (see the Appendix for a list of the team members). The BPAT conducted its evaluation in the area where most of the severe damage was concentrated: along a 200-mile stretch of Florida's Gulf of Mexico shoreline, between Pensacola Beach, in Escambia County, and St. Joseph Spit, in Gulf County (see Figure 1-1). The BPAT's observations focused on the performance of buildings during the hurricane, including both successes and failures. These observations and the BPAT's recommendations are documented in this report.

Preliminary estimates by the insurance industry indicate that Opal may be one of the most costly natural disasters to affect the United States (ranking only behind Hurricane Andrew; the Northridge, California, earthquake; and Hurricane Hugo). According to State of Florida estimates, more structures were damaged or destroyed by the effects of flooding and erosion during Hurricane Opal than in all other coastal storms affecting Florida in the past 20 years combined.

Most of the structural damage associated with the storm appeared to have been caused by coastal flood forces — storm surge, wind-generated waves, flood-induced erosion, and floodborne debris. Wind damage along the coast was confined primarily to roof damage, sign damage, tree damage, and similar impacts and was judged by the BPAT to be less severe and less extensive than flood damage.

Construction along and near the shoreline in the study area was generally governed by one or more of the following:

- The Standard Building Code, enforced by local or county governments

- National Flood Insurance Program (NFIP) construction requirements — in identified Special Flood Hazard Areas — enforced by local or county governments

- State construction requirements for structures seaward of the Coastal Construction Control Line, enforced by the Florida Department of Environmental Protection

To participate in the NFIP, a community must adopt and enforce a floodplain management ordinance based on the Flood Insurance Rate Map (FIRM) issued for the community by FEMA. The communities in the study area include structures built before the adoption of the floodplain management ordinance and structures built after the adoption of the ordinance. The former are referred to as "pre-FIRM" structures, the later as "post-FIRM." Typical pre-FIRM structures in the study area are one-story concrete block or wood-frame structures built on slab-on-grade foundations, one- to three-story concrete block structures, and one- to three-story wood-frame structures founded on timber piles. Many of these structures were behind concrete sheetpile seawalls. Typical post-FIRM structures in the study area are one-, two-, and three-story wood-frame structures elevated on timber or concrete pile foundations. Post-FIRM structures, although sustaining damage, performed much better than the pre-FIRM structures.

FLOOD DAMAGE AND VULNERABLE COMPONENTS

Because most of the structural damage observed by the BPAT along the Gulf of Mexico shoreline appeared to have been caused by flood forces rather than wind forces, the team focused on flood-induced damage. The observations of the team presented in this report address following issues:

- storm-induced erosion and scour
- debris flow and impact
- slab foundations
- pile and pier foundations
- framing systems
- connections
- bracing
- breakaway construction and enclosures below elevated buildings
- stairs, decks, and porches
- utilities
- seawalls
- drainage and drainage structures

Other issues discussed in this report include (1) the incorporation of pre-FIRM construction into new construction during the improvement of existing structures and (2) structures that appear to have been built without the aid of detailed plans prepared by a design professional. The BPAT found that poor workmanship frequently accompanied the lack of professional design in such instances.

RECOMMENDATIONS

The BPAT developed recommendations that address observed damages and vulnerabilities for both new construction and substantial improvements to existing structures in areas subject to coastal and hurricane storm forces. These recommendations include the following:

- Restudies and FIRM revisions now underway for the affected communities will use updated V-Zone mapping procedures and may result in more extensive areas being shown as V-Zones. Consequently, until such time as revised FIRMs are completed, the affected communities should consider studying local coastal flooding conditions that occurred during Hurricane Opal to determine whether areas shown as coastal A-Zones on the current FIRMs, as well as areas within several hundred feet of the Gulf of Mexico shoreline, are actually subject to V-Zone flood forces. If such areas are identified, the affected communities should strongly encourage the owners of new construction and substantial improvements to existing structures within those areas to conform with V-Zone construction standards. In addition, if areas shown as A-Zones on the current FIRMs are determined to be subject to V-Zone forces, the BFEs shown for those areas are likely to increase. Therefore, communities should also strongly encourage the owners of new construction and substantial improvements to existing structures in such areas to construct the lowest floors of their structures several feet above the BFEs shown on the current FIRMs.

- For all areas known to be subject to high-velocity wave action, strong currents, erosion, or combinations thereof — regardless of flood zone designation — the embedment depths specified for pile foundations should be sufficient to ensure that the foundation will withstand anticipated erosion and storm forces. Foundations for masonry columns should be designed to withstand all anticipated flood, erosion, debris, and wind forces. Shallow footings should not be used to support masonry columns where the risk of undermining exists.

- In areas subject to storm-induced erosion, regardless of the flood zone designation, any slabs serving as floors for habitable spaces should be designed and constructed as structural slabs, to withstand all anticipated erosion, scour, and storm forces, and attached to sufficient foundation systems that do not rely on underlying soil for support.

- In areas subject to storm-induced erosion, regardless of the flood zone designation, slabs used solely for parking should not be attached to structural members and should be designed and constructed to break into small pieces in the event of undermining, thereby minimizing potential transfer of flood loads to the structure.

- All materials should meet or exceed the minimum requirements for building materials in the Standard Building Code and FEMA's Technical Bulletin 2-93, *Flood-Resistant Materials Requirements for Buildings Located in Special Flood Hazard Areas* (FEMA 1993b).

- Repairs of damaged structures should be completed in accordance with applicable Federal, State, and local codes and regulations and should be inspected to ensure conformance with building codes and floodplain management requirements.

- Engineered plans signed and sealed by a registered design professional should be provided for both new construction and substantial improvements to existing structures in areas subject to coastal storm forces. Siting and construction in 100-year coastal flood hazard areas must meet (and, if possible, exceed) setback and elevation requirements.

This report includes photographs taken by the BPAT during the site visit. Also included are engineering design drawings that provide details which can be used to enhance building performance under hurricane and coastal flood conditions.

1 Introduction

1.1 PURPOSE

This report presents the findings of the Building Performance Assessment Team (BPAT) regarding building successes and failures during Hurricane Opal and recommends mitigation measures that will enhance the performance of buildings in future storms. The Appendix lists the BPAT members.

Typical construction types are defined for structures built prior to and after the affected communities' adoption of the floodplain management ordinance required for participation in the National Flood Insurance Program (NFIP). Because the ordinance is based on flood hazard information shown on the Flood Insurance Rate Map (FIRM) issued for each community, these structures are referred to as "pre-FIRM" and "post-FIRM," respectively. The BPAT's observations regarding flood and wind damage caused by the storm are described in detail, and recommendations are presented regarding design and construction of new structures and substantial improvements to existing structures; permitting, plan review, and inspection; construction materials; and repair and retrofit of damaged structures.

1.2 BACKGROUND

Hurricane Opal made landfall on Santa Rosa Island, in Santa Rosa County, Florida, near Navarre Beach, at approximately 6:00 p.m. c.d.t. (central daylight time) on Wednesday, October 4, 1995. Fifteen counties in the Florida Panhandle were declared Federal disaster areas (see Figure 1-1). Most of the damage was concentrated in six counties: Escambia, Santa Rosa, Okaloosa, Walton, Bay, and Gulf. Lee County, along the gulf coast in southwest Florida, was declared a Federal disaster area because of rainfall-induced flooding associated with the same storm system.

The most severe damage caused by Opal was concentrated along a 200-mile stretch of Florida's Gulf of Mexico shoreline, between Pensacola Beach (Escambia County) and St. Joseph Spit (Gulf County). This is the area where the BPAT conducted its field inspections (see Figure 1-1). The results of these inspections and the BPAT's review of post-storm video taken by the Florida Department of Environmental Protection (FDEP), Bureau of Beaches and Coastal Systems, led to the conclusion that most of the structural damage associated with the storm was caused by coastal flood forces — storm surge, wind-generated waves, storm-induced erosion, and floodborne debris. Flood damage also occurred along the shorelines of Santa Rosa Sound, Choctawhatchee Bay, and other inland waters.

Wind damage along the coast was confined largely to roof damage, sign damage, tree damage, and similar impacts and was judged by the BPAT to be less severe and less extensive than the flood damage. However, wind damage extended throughout the affected counties. Newspaper accounts indicated that approximately 18,000 dwelling units (e.g., homes, apartments, hotel/motel units) in 10 panhandle counties were rendered uninhabitable by Hurricane Opal and approximately one-fifth of these units were destroyed (*Panama City News Herald* 1995). The BPAT was unable to confirm these estimates.

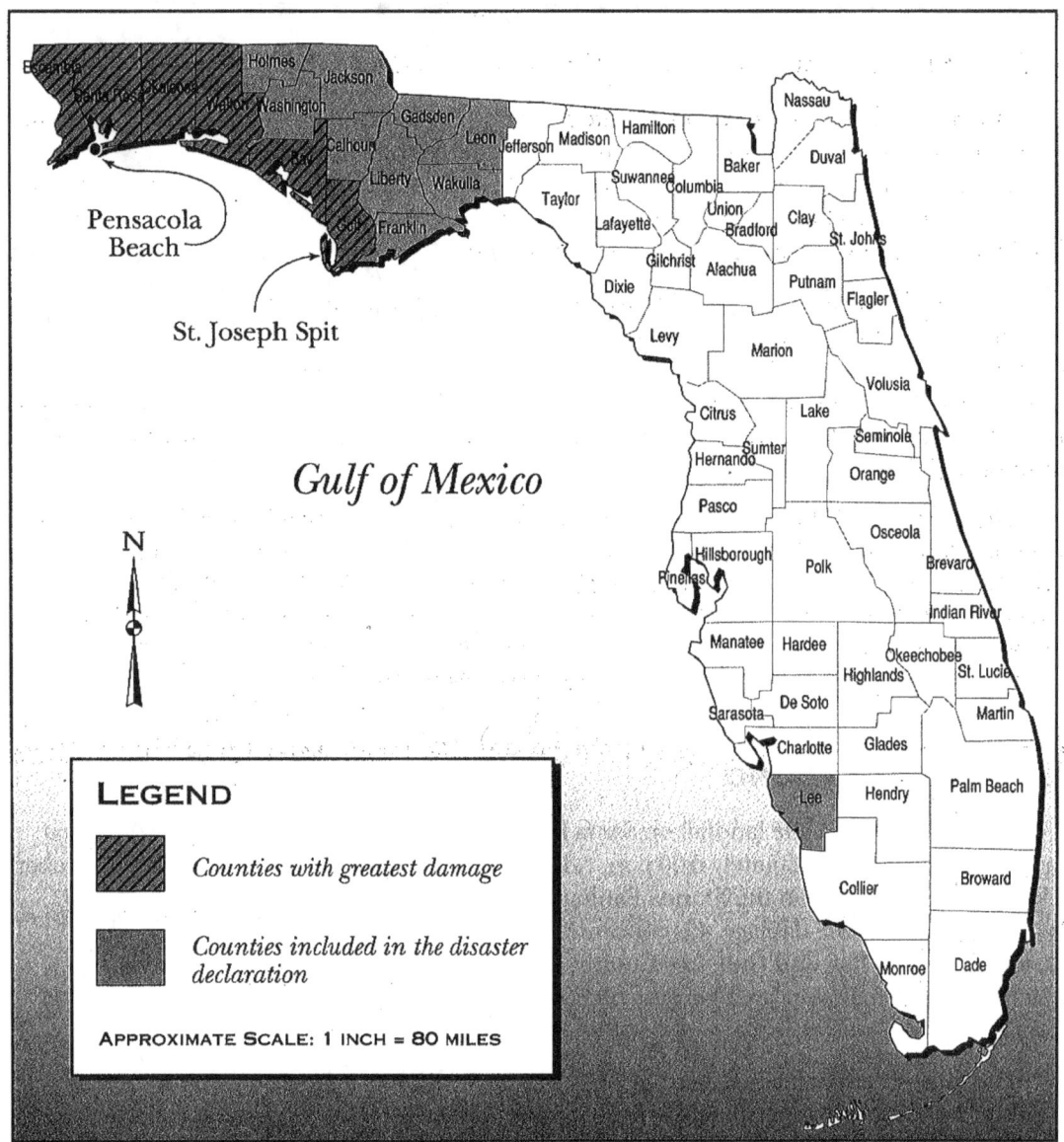

Figure 1-1   Florida counties included in the Hurricane Opal Federal disaster declaration.

Data from the FDEP (1995) indicate that approximately 990 coastal structures along the Gulf of Mexico shoreline incurred 50 percent or more damage (i.e., substantial damage). This total includes over 500 single-family dwellings and over 300 multi-family structures (containing 1,000 dwelling units and 800 motel/hotel units). The FDEP data also show that over 3 miles of concrete and timber bulkheads and retaining walls were damaged or destroyed. According to State of Florida estimates, more structures were damaged or destroyed by the effects of flooding and erosion during Hurricane Opal than in all other coastal storms affecting Florida in the past 20 years combined.

Preliminary estimates from the insurance industry show total insured losses from wind damage from the storm to be approximately $2 billion, making Opal one of the most costly natural disasters to affect the United States (ranking only behind Hurricane Andrew; the Northridge, California, earthquake; and Hurricane Hugo).

1.3   HURRICANE OPAL — STORM CONDITIONS

Hurricane Opal was classified as a Category 3 storm on the Saffir-Simpson scale at the time of landfall, with a central pressure of 940 millibars (mb) and recorded sustained wind speeds of approximately 110 to 115 miles per hour (mph). Recorded wind speeds rapidly decayed to 86 to 92 mph just inland. The storm was moving north-northeast with a forward speed of 22 mph at landfall (National Oceanic and Atmospheric Administration 1995).

Water level data from a National Oceanic and Atmospheric Administration (NOAA) tide gage on the Panama City Beach pier show a peak water level of approximately 8.5 feet above Mean Lower Low Water (MLLW) at 6:00 p.m. c.d.t., nearly 8 feet above the predicted astronomical tide. Water level data from the NOAA gage at Apalachicola show a peak water level of approximately 6.6 feet MLLW at 7:30 p.m. c.d.t., approximately 6 feet above the predicted astronomical tide.

High-water mark surveys conducted after Hurricane Opal (Michael Baker, Jr. 1995) show that water levels ranged from approximately 8 to 11 feet National Geodetic Vertical Datum (NGVD) along Santa Rosa Island between Pensacola Beach and Fort Walton Beach, approximately 12 to 20 feet NGVD between Destin and Seagrove Beach, and approximately 8 to 12 feet NGVD along Panama City Beach.

1.4   LOCAL, STATE, AND FEDERAL SITING AND BUILDING CODE REQUIREMENTS

Construction along and near the shoreline in the study area was generally governed by one or more of the following: the Standard Building Code, enforced by local or county governments; NFIP construction requirements — in identified Special Flood Hazard Areas — enforced by local or county governments; and State construction requirements for structures seaward of the Coastal Construction Control Line (CCCL), enforced by FDEP, Bureau of Beaches and Coastal Systems (formerly known as the Florida Department of Natural Resources, Division of Beaches and Shores).

FIRMs which show Base Flood Elevations (BFEs) that include wave height effects were adopted by communities in the study area between June 1983 and August 1987. (The base flood, also referred to as the 100-year flood, is the flood that has a 1-percent probability of being equaled or exceeded in any given year and is the basis for the regulatory requirements of the NFIP.) Because the NFIP Flood Insurance Studies on which the FIRMs are based were completed at different times, during which V-Zone mapping criteria were evolving, some of the studies accounted for wave setup, wave runup, and erosion, and others did not.

The Flood Insurance Studies indicate that the predicted 100-year stillwater (or storm surge) elevations along the majority of the Gulf of Mexico shoreline in the study area range from 4 feet to 6 feet NGVD. In the same area, V-Zones generally range from 100 to 300 feet in width and the wave crest elevations in the V-Zone range from 7 to 9 feet NGVD. Higher elevations are indicated for the Pensacola Beach and Perdido Key areas, where the predicted 100-year stillwater elevations range from 8 feet to 12 feet NGVD, V-Zones range from 200 to 400 feet in width, and V-Zone wave crest elevations range from 12 to 15 feet NGVD.

The State of Florida established the CCCL along Florida's sandy beach shorelines to delineate those areas subject to erosion or other adverse impacts during a 100-year storm. Specific elevation and construction requirements are enforced by the State seaward of the CCCL. With the exception of Bay County, the portions of the CCCL in the study area were adopted by the State between 1982 and 1991 and reflect anticipated 100-year storm impact zones. However, the pre-Opal CCCL in Bay County was essentially unchanged from a 50-foot setback line established by the State in 1975 and did not include all areas subject to 100-year storm impacts. After Hurricane Opal, the State adopted a revised CCCL for Bay County on an emergency basis. The new line is 100 feet landward of the pre-Opal line and became effective on October 16, 1995. Reconstruction of many damaged or destroyed structures along the Bay County shoreline will now be subject to CCCL construction requirements.

The FDEP has also completed its own studies that predict 100-year stillwater elevations along the Gulf of Mexico shoreline. FDEP studies for the reach between Escambia and Bay Counties generally show 100-year stillwater elevations ranging between 11 feet and 12 feet NGVD. The 5-foot to 6-foot difference between FDEP and NFIP 100-year stillwater levels is attributed to the inclusion of dynamic wave setup by FDEP.

A comparison of V-Zone boundaries and the location of the State's CCCL had not been completed at the time this report was prepared (a comparison is expected by late 1996). However, the State's foundation and elevation requirements seaward of the CCCL (i.e., pile penetration requirements and lowest floor elevations) are known to be more stringent than NFIP V-Zone requirements. Likewise, the State's wind load requirements seaward of the CCCL are known to be more stringent than the wind load requirements of the Standard Building Code. According to the FDEP (1995), no major habitable structures located seaward of the CCCL and permitted by the State under current standards sustained significant structural damage during Hurricane Opal. In contrast, the FDEP reported that over one-half of the pre-existing major habitable structures seaward of the CCCL (i.e., structures either not permitted by the State or constructed prior to State permitting requirements) sustained structural damage during the storm.

2 Site Observations

2.1 TYPICAL PRE-FIRM AND POST-FIRM CONSTRUCTION

Typical pre-FIRM structures in the study area are one-story concrete block or wood-frame structures built on slab-on-grade foundations, one- to three-story concrete block structures, and one- to three-story wood-frame structures founded on timber piles. Many of these structures are behind concrete sheetpile seawalls. Many pre-FIRM structures were substantially damaged by the surge accompanying the storm event and were often destroyed because of foundation collapse, wave attack, or both.

Typical post-FIRM structures in the study area are one-, two-, and three-story wood-frame structures elevated on timber or concrete pile foundations. Some of these are new structures that either incorporate older, pre-FIRM structures or were built over them. Post-FIRM elevated structures sustained some wind and flood damage but, overall, performed much better than pre-FIRM structures that were at-grade or that were elevated but not to the BFE or CCCL requirements.

2.2 OBSERVATIONS OF WIND DAMAGE

Wind damage observed by the BPAT was generally confined to roofing shingles and tiles, exterior sheathing, unsecured air conditioning compressors, power poles and lines, and signs. However, the wind damage observed did not constitute a large portion of the total damage to structures.

2.3 OBSERVATIONS OF FLOOD DAMAGE

Flood damage was observed along the Gulf of Mexico shoreline at all sites visited by the BPAT (see Figures 2-1 and 2-2). Structures damaged by flood forces generally fell into the following categories:

- pre-FIRM structures founded on slabs or shallow footings and located in mapped V-Zones

- post-FIRM structures in mapped A-Zones, B-Zones, C-Zones, and X-Zones founded on slabs or shallow footings, but exposed to high-velocity flows, high-velocity wave action, flood-induced erosion, floodborne debris, or burial by overwash

- post-FIRM elevated structures not properly constructed or not elevated to or above the elevation reached by storm surge and wave effects

- pre- and post-FIRM structures dependent, in part or completely, on failed seawalls or bulkheads for protection and foundation support.

Figure 2-1   Debris washed inland as a result of surge action from Hurricane Opal (note circled boats).

Figure 2-2   Beach erosion caused major damage to structures, as well as roads and utilities.

2.3.1 EROSION AND SCOUR

Where sand dunes existed before Hurricane Opal, significant loss of dune height and width was observed. Many dunes were breached or flattened (see Figure 2-3). Those that remained after the storm were scarped and weakened. Duneface retreat of 75 feet to 100 feet was observed in several locations. Overwash of eroded dune sediments was common, sometimes extending over 500 feet inland and causing burial of roads and at-grade construction by 1 to 4 feet of sand.

In some cases, an estimated 10 to 20 feet of vertical relief was lost at the seaward edge of high dune and bluff areas. Many structures atop high dunes or bluffs collapsed because of a loss of support, either from the undermining of slab foundations or from inadequate pile embedment (see Figure 2-4).

Ground levels at many front-row elevated structures that survived Hurricane Opal were typically reduced 3 to 7 feet, or more. In addition, local scour depressions were observed at the bases of many piles, indicating that 6 to 12 inches of additional soil was lost immediately adjacent to the piles. Scour during the storm probably rendered greater than 6 to 12 inches of soil around the piles unsupporting.

Large scour depressions were observed where large volumes of water flowed during the storm. Depressions measuring 10 to 40 feet in length and width and 2 to 4 feet in depth were observed around some pile-supported structures and near the corners of some at-grade construction. Structures that seemed particularly vulnerable included the following:

- structures at the landward termination of roads and driveways that funneled floodwaters toward the structures

- structures between drainage basins or lakes and larger bodies of water

- structures near locations where floodwaters crossed or breached the barrier islands

2.3.2 DEBRIS

Small debris was widespread, ranging from household items to construction materials. These items did not cause structural damage to buildings, foundations, or other building components. Evidence of much larger debris shifted by floodwaters was also observed, including pier piles and braces, concrete slabs, dumpsters, automobiles, boats, and collapsed houses (see Figure 2-5). Many of these objects washed into buildings, and some caused structural damage.

2.3.3 SLAB FOUNDATIONS

Many slab failures were noted in all types of structures (see Figure 2-6). The major reason for these failures was the loss of support coupled with a lack of reinforcing in the slabs. Welded reinforcing wire fabric was observed in many slabs but did not prevent failure of the slabs once they were undermined.

Figure 2-3   *Beach erosion eliminated protection for structures. It is important that the beach and dunes be rebuilt as soon as possible. Arrows point to walkways used to traverse dune that has been washed away.*

Figure 2-4   *Erosion such as this took place along the gulf coast, causing structures to be undermined and resulting in damage.*

Figure 2-5   Debris, consisting of broken concrete and wood framing systems, generated by surge action.

Figure 2-6   Undermining of concrete decks and floor slabs caused the failure of many unreinforced concrete structures.

2.3.4 Pile and Pier Foundations

Three to seven feet of vertical erosion at the seaward row of piles was common (see Figure 2-7). This erosion, coupled with insufficient penetration of the piles on many structures, led to structural damage to or collapse of primarily pre-FIRM structures. Undersized piles (6-inch diameter timber in some instances) were not sufficient to resist storm forces; they generally failed and resulted in structural damage or collapse. Piers constructed of concrete blocks on shallow footings frequently collapsed as a result of erosion. Well-designed and well-constructed pile and pier foundations withstood the forces exerted by the storm. Use of splicing techniques was also observed on some eroded piles (see Figure 2-8). Although the splicing of piles placed these structures at increased risk of failure, no failures related to spliced piles were observed.

2.3.5 Framing Systems

The BPAT found many examples of poor framing of timber floor beams and joists in platform-type construction. In particular, poorly fashioned beam-to-beam and joist-to-beam connections were common. Typical problems included the following:

- pile notching greater than 50 percent of pile cross-section
- poor alignment of piles, which resulted in unsupported beams at piles
- use of wooden shims to support beams (i.e., to compensate for notches cut too low)
- overreliance on nails and thin metal straps/hangers

Glue-laminated beams and joists were observed in exterior applications in some recent post-FIRM residential construction. The use of laminated structural members in exterior applications

Distance to Eroded
Beach Elevation

Figure 2-7   These piles were not embedded deep enough to survive the erosion of the sand. As a result, there is now a large gap between the bottoms of the pilings and the ground surface.

is of interest because this practice has not been widely observed by previous BPATs. Although laminated structural members rated for exterior use are available, the Hurricane Opal BPAT could not determine the rating of those it saw. No failures of these beams and joists were observed however.

2.3.6 CONNECTIONS

Many of the connections observed were deficient. The BPAT observed widespread corrosion of galvanized straps, hangers, and joist-to-beam ties beneath elevated buildings. Some of the corroded connectors had failed either before or during the storm.

The BPAT observed some galvanized strap connectors between piles, beams and joists (in otherwise good condition) that failed as a result of insufficient nailing or because storm forces exceeded the design forces (see Figure 2-9). This was not a common mode of failure, however. The BPAT also found evidence that structural components had pulled away from one another when acted on simultaneously by flood and wind forces, despite the presence of the galvanized connectors. In some instances, foundation piles and beams were well-connected and withstood storm forces, while walls or upper structure components were poorly connected and were damaged or destroyed by wind forces, flood forces, or both.

2.3.7 BRACING

The use of 2 x 8 or similar timber cross-bracing between timber piles was common beneath elevated wood-frame structures. Some bracing failures were observed that were apparently due to horizontal loading from water, debris, or both. The use of threaded galvanized rods and turnbuckles as cross-bracing was less common (see Figure 2-10). No failures of this type of bracing

Figure 2-8   These piles were not long enough and were spliced to add depth. The splicing was exposed by storm-induced erosion.

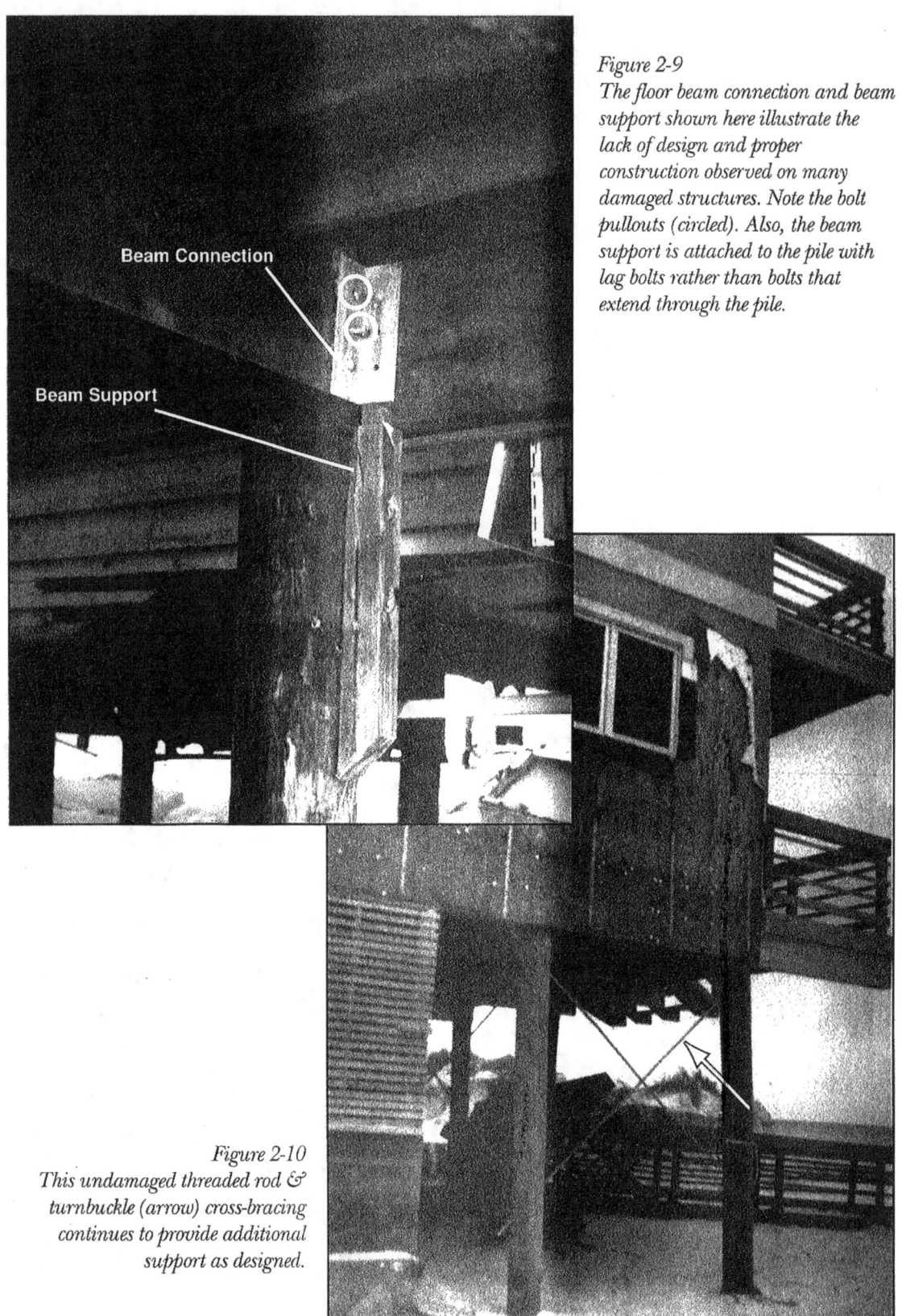

Beam Connection

Beam Support

Figure 2-9
The floor beam connection and beam support shown here illustrate the lack of design and proper construction observed on many damaged structures. Note the bolt pullouts (circled). Also, the beam support is attached to the pile with lag bolts rather than bolts that extend through the pile.

Figure 2-10
This undamaged threaded rod & turnbuckle (arrow) cross-bracing continues to provide additional support as designed.

were noted, but debris was trapped by the bracing, and in some instances, the rods were bent by lateral loads imposed by the force of flood waters acting on the trapped debris.

Use of knee bracing was also prevalent in elevated wood-frame structures. A common problem observed with knee bracing was that timber piles had been notched, some deeply, to accommodate bearing seats for tie-in purposes. Although the BPAT did not observe any structural failures that could be definitively linked to this problem, notching of piles can undermine their structural integrity and should therefore be avoided.

2.3.8 BREAKAWAY CONSTRUCTION AND ENCLOSURES

There were a number of damaged or destroyed enclosures below elevated structures (see Figure 2-11), many with electrical wiring attached to breakaway walls. The presence of breakaway walls indicates the designer was aware of potential flood impacts. However, the placement or attachment of utilities to breakaway walls below the elevated portions of the structures demonstrates, at a minimum, lack of awareness of local, CCCL, and NFIP regulations by owners or contractors, or possibly disregard of those regulations.

In some post-FIRM structures with breakaway walls below the lowest habitable floor, the walls broke away as intended but in doing so, damaged exterior sheathing and wall finishes above the lowest floor. The damage above the breakaway wall was usually minor but could have been prevented by better design and construction of this detail (as shown in Figure 2-11). Rolldown garage doors were damaged or destroyed in pre-FIRM and post-FIRM construction alike (see Figure 2-11).

2.3.9 STAIRS, DECKS, AND PORCHES

Timber stairs and decks were frequent casualties of the storm. Many were supported by short, small-diameter shallow posts or piles. Some decks were supported by knee braces attached to structural piles supporting the main structure. Decks of this design seemed to better resist Opal's forces. Loss of decks sometimes led to roof damage where roof overhangs were supported by posts attached to the decks. In one instance, a deck located seaward of the State's CCCL and permitted by the State survived the storm, while the landward habitable structure (behind the CCCL and not within the State's jurisdiction) was destroyed.

2.3.10 UTILITIES

The BPAT noted several problems associated with utilities and utility connections at habitable structures:

- Placement of electric meters, panels, boxes, and wiring below a building's lowest habitable floor, rendering that equipment vulnerable to storm surge, wave, debris and overwash damage (see Figure 2-12).

- Attachment of wiring, conduit, and electrical panels to breakaway walls (see Figure 2-13).

- Failure to adequately support and fasten air conditioning compressor units (see Figure 2-14). Many support platforms were destroyed, leading to compressor damage. Some platforms survived, while unfastened compressor units were blown or washed away. Units not properly supported and attached were also observed to have caused damage to exterior walls of some structures.

- Placement of utility lines, septic systems, and mechanical connections and equipment, including air conditioning units, on the sides or seaward of buildings, rather than landward of the building. Loss of air conditioning units and/or utility/mechanical components sometimes led to damage of the main structure.

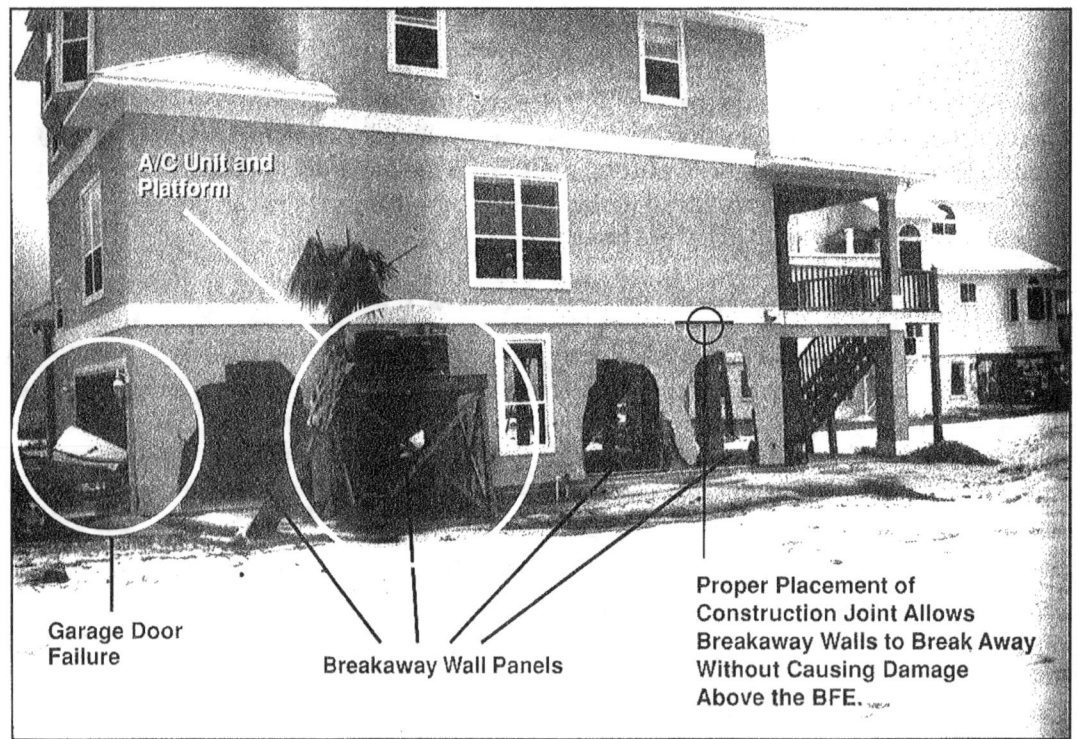

A/C Unit and
Platform

Garage Door
Failure

Breakaway Wall Panels

Proper Placement of
Construction Joint Allows
Breakaway Walls to Break Away
Without Causing Damage
Above the BFE.

*Figure 2-11   These breakaway walls functioned as designed, lessening the pressures of water, sand, and
debris on the structure.*

*Figure 2-12   Utility lines and boxes dislocated by hurricane forces. Note that the cross-bracing and pile
support system remain in good condition after the storm.*

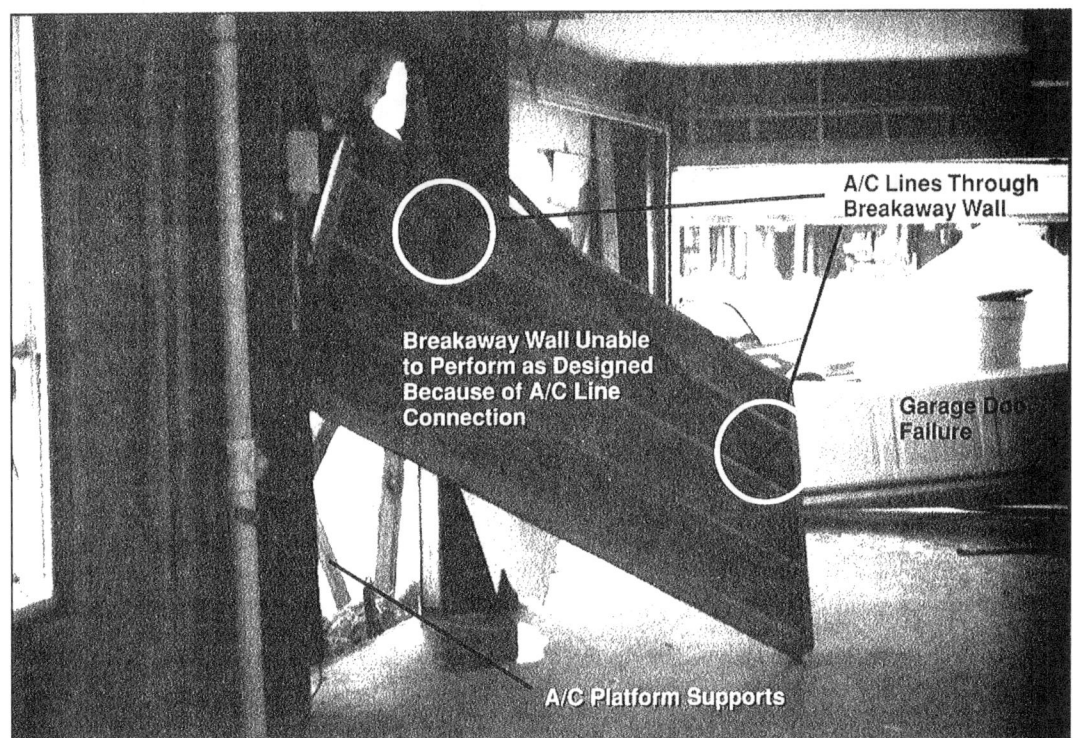

Figure 2-13   Interior view of breakaway wall blocked by air conditioning unit and support platform (see Figure 2-11). Electric and cooling lines were extended through the breakaway panel.

Figure 2-14   These breakaway panels functioned as designed. Note the loss of the air conditioning unit platform.

2.3.11 SEAWALLS

The BPAT observed widespread failure of seawalls and bulkheads along the Gulf of Mexico shoreline (see Figure 2-15). Damage figures from the State of Florida revealed that over 3 miles of seawalls and bulkheads were destroyed by Hurricane Opal, including 1.3 miles of concrete walls, 1.0 mile of concrete block walls, and 0.8 mile of timber walls (FDEP 1995). Failed walls contributed to damage of buildings, pools, and other structures, due to loss of backfill and generation of debris.

Many walls appeared to have failed because wing walls or return walls were flanked by erosion and scour. Many seawall returns flanked by erosion and scour were no more than 20 to 30 feet long, although some longer returns (50 feet to 75 feet) were also flanked.

Seawalls were usually destroyed when backfill was washed from behind the walls because of overtopping, insufficient wall embedment, or return wall flanking. Habitable structures founded on slabs or shallow foundations, swimming pools, and other structures that relied on seawalls to retain supporting soil, were frequently undermined and destroyed when seawalls failed.

The BPAT noted that retaining walls constructed of concrete blocks were particularly vulnerable to damage by Hurricane Opal. Walls most likely to have survived were observed to have:

- reinforced concrete slab or sheetpile construction

- sufficient wall height or backfill protection to prevent significant overtopping and loss of backfill

Figure 2-15   Fractured seawall, damaged by storm forces. Note the erosion of the bank behind the wall.

- sufficient anchorage and embedment to prevent collapse from seaward rotation of the cap or toe

- return walls extending landward of the seaward face of the building or structure being protected and landward of the effects of erosion and scour

2.3.12 DRAINAGE AND DRAINAGE STRUCTURES

The BPAT observed the remains of several new stormwater discharge structures adjacent to or between multifamily buildings. These structures consisted of large-diameter corrugated plastic pipes, probably intended to carry stormwater runoff from parking areas and other impervious areas to the beach. Unfortunately, the seaward portions of these pipes were destroyed during the storm and their pre-storm configurations are not known with certainty.

It did appear, however, that erosion beneath habitable structures near these damaged discharge pipes was more severe than at areas away from the pipes, possibly a result of direct discharge of upland stormwater runoff adjacent to or beneath the habitable structures. It is likely that the pipes failed because of erosion and scour caused by the storm or because of the loss of protective seawalls and bulkheads. It is possible, but not known for certain, that the pipe failures and discharge adjacent to the multifamily buildings contributed to foundation damage at those buildings.

2.4 INCORPORATION OF PRE-FIRM CONSTRUCTION INTO NEW CONSTRUCTION

Many single-family structures appeared to have been constructed above or adjacent to portions of older pre-FIRM structures and probably resulted from efforts to expand and/or reconstruct older, smaller structures. This type of construction is vulnerable to storm damage because the foundations of the pre-FIRM and post-FIRM sections can respond differently to storm forces and erosion. For example, the BPAT found a damaged house in Mexico Beach that was supported by two types of foundations. One part of the house was supported on concrete block piers placed on the old pre-FIRM slab-on-grade. The remainder of the house, which extended beyond the original pre-FIRM footprint, was supported on timber piles set in concrete encasements. Although the piles and slab survived the storm, the concrete block piers did not. With the loss of the piers, the house listed to the unsupported side and the floor beams separated from the newer, pile foundation. Had the entire house been supported on timber piles, it may have survived with little or no damage.

2.5 DESIGN, CONSTRUCTION, AND WORKMANSHIP

After observing hundreds of damaged or destroyed structures, the BPAT has concluded that many structures seem either to have been built without the aid of detailed design plans (prepared by a design professional) or not to have been built in accordance with plans that were available. Failure of non-engineered or poorly designed foundations, structural systems, and critical connections often led to major damage or complete loss of structures. Such losses are preventable.

Numerous instances of poor workmanship were also noted by the BPAT during its inspections. In particular, the BPAT found several examples of misalignment of timber foundation piles and poor framing practices in platform-type construction. The BPAT also noted recurring problems with concrete construction. For example, reinforcing steel was missing from or misplaced in slabs, footers, and wall grade beams, and welded wire fabric reinforcement was frequently at the bottom of, not centered in, the slabs. Although no damage was observed that could be definitively linked to these examples of poor workmanship, such practices should be avoided in any construction, especially in areas subject to coastal storm forces.

3 Recommendations

The BPAT's recommendations are presented below. Engineering design drawings are also presented that illustrate the recommendations and provide details that can be used to enhance building performance under hurricane and coastal flood conditions.

3.1 APPLICATION OF V-ZONE AND A-ZONE DESIGN AND CONSTRUCTION REQUIREMENTS

NFIP V-Zone construction requirements specify that new construction be elevated on piles, posts, columns, or piers and that the bottom of the lowest horizontal structural member (e.g., floor beam, joist) be at or above the BFE. Depending on the dimensions of those structural members, the resulting lowest floor elevations can be as much as 1.5 feet above the BFE. By comparison, NFIP A-Zone standards for new construction require that the lowest floor of the structure be at or above the BFE.

FIRMs accounting for wave effects were adopted by the communities in the study area between 1985 and 1987, prior to changes in V-Zone mapping procedures that extended coastal V-Zones to the landward toe of the primary frontal dune. The BPAT believes that this factor, coupled with a decade of long-term erosion, resulted in narrow V-Zones and an underestimation of actual risk along or near the shoreline, which increased the exposure of some post-FIRM A-Zone construction to V-Zone flood forces.

3.1.1 FEMA TO ISSUE REVISED FIRMS

FEMA will address the V-Zone issue discussed above by completing restudies and revisions to the FIRMs as necessary for the communities in the study area. Preliminary revised maps for the affected communities will not be completed until 1997; thus, the majority of post-Opal reconstruction will be governed by the FIRMs in effect at the time of the storm and by State CCCL requirements. Until the revised FIRMs are completed, the affected communities should consider studying local coastal flooding conditions that occurred during Hurricane Opal to determine whether areas in coastal A-Zones, as well as areas within several hundred feet of the Gulf of Mexico shoreline, are actually subject to V-Zone flood forces. If such areas are identified, the affected communities should strongly encourage the owners of new construction and substantial improvements to existing structures within those areas to conform with V-Zone construction standards and to provide several feet of freeboard above the BFEs shown on the current FIRMs.

3.1.2 COMMUNITIES USING HIGHER STANDARDS IN COASTAL A-ZONES

The benefit of applying more stringent requirements to new construction in coastal A-Zones in the study area was illustrated by the performance of recent post-FIRM A-Zone construction in the City of Pensacola Beach during Hurricane Opal. Under the jurisdiction of the Santa Rosa Island Authority (SRIA), the city enforces V-Zone construction standards in all of the barrier island areas shown as A-Zones on its current FIRM. Within the same A-Zones, the SRIA also requires that the lowest horizontal structural member of all new construction be at or above an elevation of 10 feet NGVD. Therefore, the lowest floor elevation would be approximately 11.5 feet NGVD or higher. The A-Zone BFE ranges from a minimum of 6 feet NGVD to a maximum of 10 feet NGVD. Therefore, the SRIA's requirement results in lowest floor elevations up to 5.5 feet higher than what would otherwise be obtained. During Hurricane Opal, flooding occurred in V-Zone and A-Zone areas shown on the city's FIRM. Recent post-FIRM A-Zone construction generally performed well, as evidenced by the survival of elevated structures in A-Zones and the destruction of nearby pre-FIRM, at-grade structures. The BPAT believes that the higher elevations of lowest floors, coupled with the requirement for construction on piles, helped to significantly reduce the extent of damage in the city's barrier island A-Zones.

Communities that are considering adopting more restrictive requirements in their coastal A-Zones, such as V-Zone construction requirements or freeboard requirements, may want to contact the FEMA Region IV Office or the State of Florida Department of Community Affairs for technical assistance. Communities should also consider that by adopting these more restrictive requirements, they can earn community-wide reductions in flood insurance premiums under the NFIP's Community Rating System. In addition, lower flood insurance premiums can be obtained for individual structures when the structures are built to provide freeboard above the BFE. Such structures, if designed and constructed in accordance with the NFIP requirements, will receive lower premiums in 1-foot increments for up to 4 feet of freeboard above the BFE.

Communities are encouraged to reexamine foundation design requirements for structures in areas near the Gulf of Mexico shoreline in light of damage caused by Hurricane Opal. Structures in these areas should be designed to withstand all anticipated flood, erosion, debris, and wind forces. Foundation designs for structures in A-Zones, B-Zones, C-Zones, and X-Zones should be considered carefully to ensure that the designs reflect actual risks. Therefore, the BPAT recommends that communities and individuals consider the following:

- For all areas subject to high-velocity wave action, strong currents, erosion, or combinations thereof — regardless of flood zone designation — the embedment depths specified for pile foundations should be sufficient to ensure that the foundation will withstand anticipated erosion, conical scour, and storm forces.

- Foundations for masonry columns should be designed to withstand all anticipated flood, erosion, conical scour, debris, and wind forces. Shallow footings should not be used to support masonry columns where the risk of undermining exists.

- In areas known to be subject to storm-induced scour and erosion, any slabs serving as floors for habitable spaces should be designed and constructed to withstand all anticipated erosion, scour, and storm forces. Therefore, if the potential for undermining exists, slabs should be designed and constructed as structural slabs and attached to sufficient foundation systems that do not rely on underlying soil for support.

- In areas known to be subject to storm-induced scour and erosion, slabs used solely for parking should not be attached to structural members and should be designed and constructed to break into small pieces in the event of undermining, thereby minimizing potential transfer of flood loads to the structure.

3.2 Permitting, Plan Review, and Inspection

From the nature and extent of damage observed during its inspections, the BPAT has concluded that the quality of new construction can and should be improved. The specific recommendations of the Hurricane Opal BPAT regarding this issue, listed below, are similar to recommendations made by the BPAT that assessed damage resulting from Hurricane Andrew (FEMA 1992).

- Designers, building officials, and contractors must ensure that all anticipated storm forces are taken into consideration and must avoid practices that have led to common building failures. Most building failures are predictable from the actual performance of similar structures during previous storms. Communities may want to consider requiring designers and contractors, through certification, registration, or continuing education, to demonstrate knowledge of all anticipated storm loads (e.g., wind, flood, debris, erosion) and proper design and construction methods that enable structures to withstand those forces.

- Quality of construction workmanship should be improved. Contractors and subcontractors should construct strictly according to design plans, and they should not attempt to compensate for changed site conditions or construction flaws and errors with non-engineered adjustments and repairs. Attempts to devise and implement rapid fixes to construction problems may render a structure vulnerable to storm forces and may lead to structural damage or destruction. Field representatives of building departments should require that plans be resubmitted when such concerns are identified in the field.

- Permitting, plan review, and construction inspection procedures should be improved. The knowledge and training of reviewers and inspectors should be enhanced through certification or continuing education. Building departments would need sufficient financial and human resources to ensure that frequent and comprehensive inspections occur during construction. Plan review and construction inspection tasks should make greater use of licensed design professionals. This could be accomplished through various combinations of public and private sector responsibilities. For example, a community with adequate resources could employ design professionals to support both plan review and construction inspection. Alternatively, a community could require that engineers and architects of record assume greater responsibility for monitoring and inspecting construction. The latter approach was taken in Dade County, Florida, after the Hurricane Andrew disaster.

3.3 Construction Materials

All materials should meet or exceed the minimum requirements for building materials in the Standard Building Code. All materials subject to flooding should resist damage, deterioration, corrosion, and decay due to inundation, precipitation, wind-driven water, salt spray, or other corrosive agents. Guidance concerning flood- and corrosion-resistant materials can be found in FEMA's Technical Bulletin 2-93, *Flood-Resistant Materials Requirements* for Buildings Located in Special Flood Hazard Areas (FEMA 1993b) and Technical Bulletin 8-96, *Corrosion Protection for Metal Connectors in Coastal Areas* (FEMA 1996). For example:

- Special consideration should be given to structural connectors such as hurricane straps and hangers to ensure they are specified properly and that precautions are taken with metal structural components to ensure that structural integrity is not compromised by corrosion (FEMA 1996).

- Where used to provide structural support for elevated structures, laminated or structural composite beams and joists should be properly specified, manufactured, treated, and installed for exterior use to avoid deterioration, delamination, or other problems that may result from use of members intended for interior use. Furthermore, designers and contractors should employ connections and connectors recommended by the American Institute of Timber Construction and allowed by the local building code, since standard connections and connectors used with sawn lumber may not be appropriate for laminated or composite lumber.

- Asphalt roofing shingles should be of sufficient size and weight to meet wind resistance requirements in the applicable building code. Roofing tiles should be properly nailed, screwed, or fastened in accordance with the manufacturer's recommendations.

- Metal roofing should be properly fastened to reduce damage, which tends to be progressive — a small defect can result in loss of the entire metal roof.

3.4 REPAIR AND RETROFIT OF DAMAGED STRUCTURES

Repairs of damaged structures should be completed in accordance with applicable codes and regulations and should be inspected to ensure conformance to the applicable building code and floodplain management requirements. Designers and contractors should be reminded that if a structure is damaged to the point that the cost of repairing it to its pre-damage condition equals or exceeds 50 percent of its pre-damage market value, repair will be governed by local, State, or NFIP substantial damage regulations, as adopted by community floodplain ordinance.

Opportunities to retrofit damaged structures should also be aggressively pursued. Elevation, relocation, floodproofing, and installation of protective structures should be considered as effective means of reducing future damages (Florida Department of Community Affairs 1995). Where possible, retrofitting measures should be passive measures that do not require human intervention.

3.5 NEW CONSTRUCTION AND SUBSTANTIAL IMPROVEMENTS

In V-Zones, construction plans for all new and substantially improved structures must be signed and sealed by a registered design professional. The BPAT recommends that in coastal A-Zones, plans for new and substantially improved structures also be signed and sealed by a registered design professional. Consideration should be given to having building setbacks from the shoreline and first floor elevations exceed minimum requirements where current FIRMs and construction setbacks do not reflect the actual flood levels, erosion, scour, and storm effects experienced during Hurricane Opal.

3.5.1 PILE, POST, COLUMN, AND PIER FOUNDATIONS

Pile, post, column, and pier foundations should be designed to accommodate all design flood, wind, and other loads acting simultaneously in accordance with the requirements of ASCE 7-95, *Minimum Design Loads for Buildings and Other Structures* (ASCE 1995). Documented amounts of erosion and conical scour from Hurricane Opal and earlier storms should be considered in the determination of foundation embedment. When cast-in-place concrete piers are poured, measures should be used to prevent sand or earth from collapsing into the excavation and reducing the pier cross-section. Figure 3-1 shows the survival of a structure built on a well-constructed concrete pile foundation that sustained severe erosion. Figures 3-2 through 3-9 show recommended pile, post, column, and pier foundation designs. While there were no failures observed of spliced wood piles (see Figure 2-8), the recommended practice is to install foundation elements in a continuous length (i.e., in one piece).

3.5.2 SLABS AND GRADE BEAMS

With the exception of at-grade parking slabs, slabs-on-grade in areas known to be subject to storm-induced erosion and scour should be designed as freestanding structural elements and reinforced to withstand the loss of underlying soil. Freestanding structural slabs should be designed and constructed to withstand all flood, wind, and debris forces acting simultaneously (in accordance with applicable standards and codes) and to minimize debris trapping.

Grade beams should be designed as freestanding structural elements that are reinforced to withstand the loss of underlying soil, to withstand all flood, wind, and debris forces acting simultaneously, and to minimize debris trapping. The design of other structural components must consider the hydrodynamic and other forces that will act on grade beams and structural slabs once they are exposed to flood forces by storm-induced erosion and scour.

Pre-storm ground elevation

Figure 3-1 *This well-constructed concrete structure survived the storm with little or no damage, even with 5 feet of erosion.*

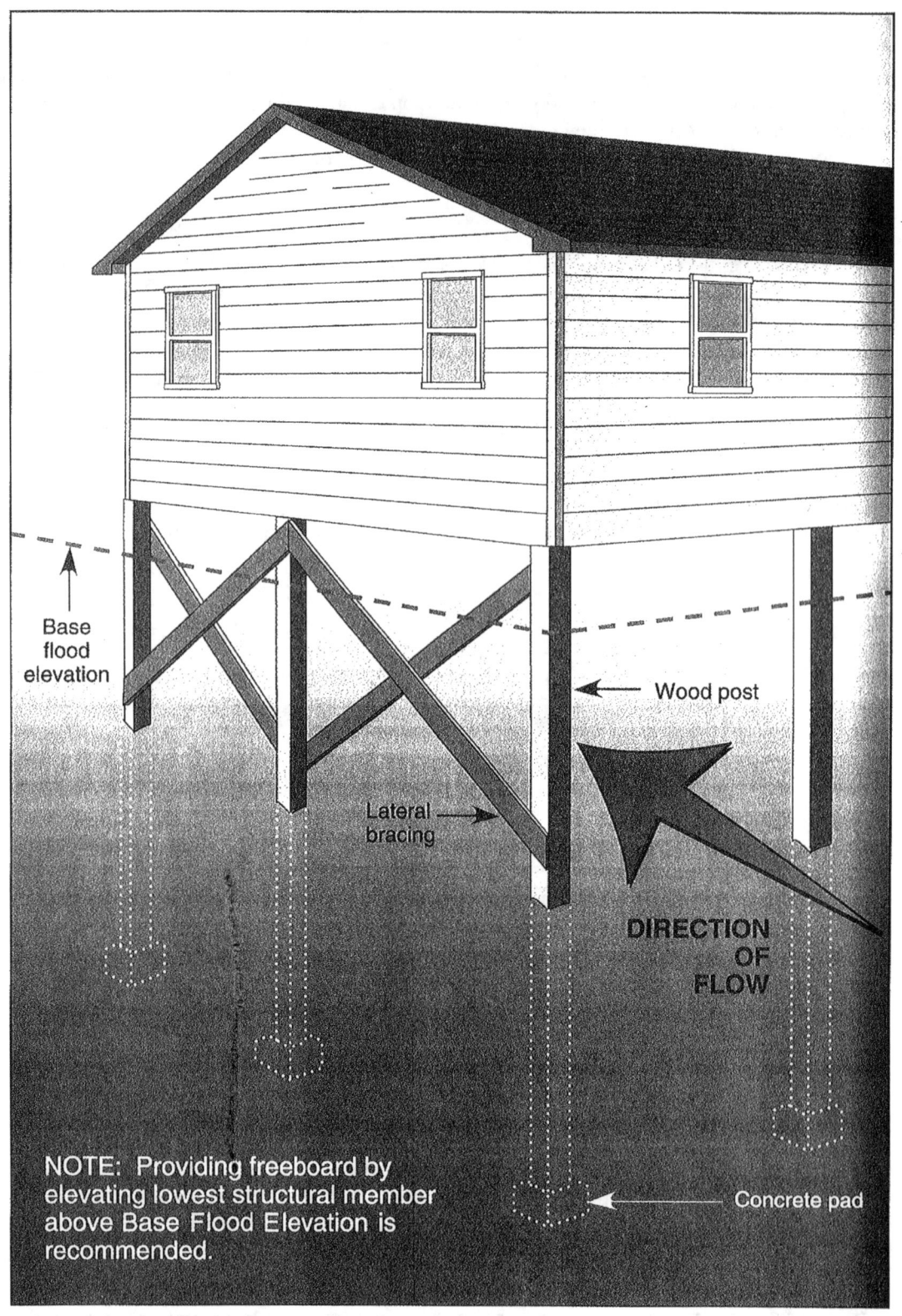

Base flood elevation

Wood post

Lateral bracing

DIRECTION OF FLOW

NOTE: Providing freeboard by elevating lowest structural member above Base Flood Elevation is recommended.

Concrete pad

Figure 3-2   Posts are placed in excavated holes and may be anchored in a concrete pad at the bottom of the hole. Where possible, lateral bracing should be oriented parallel to the anticipated flow path (FEMA 1993a).

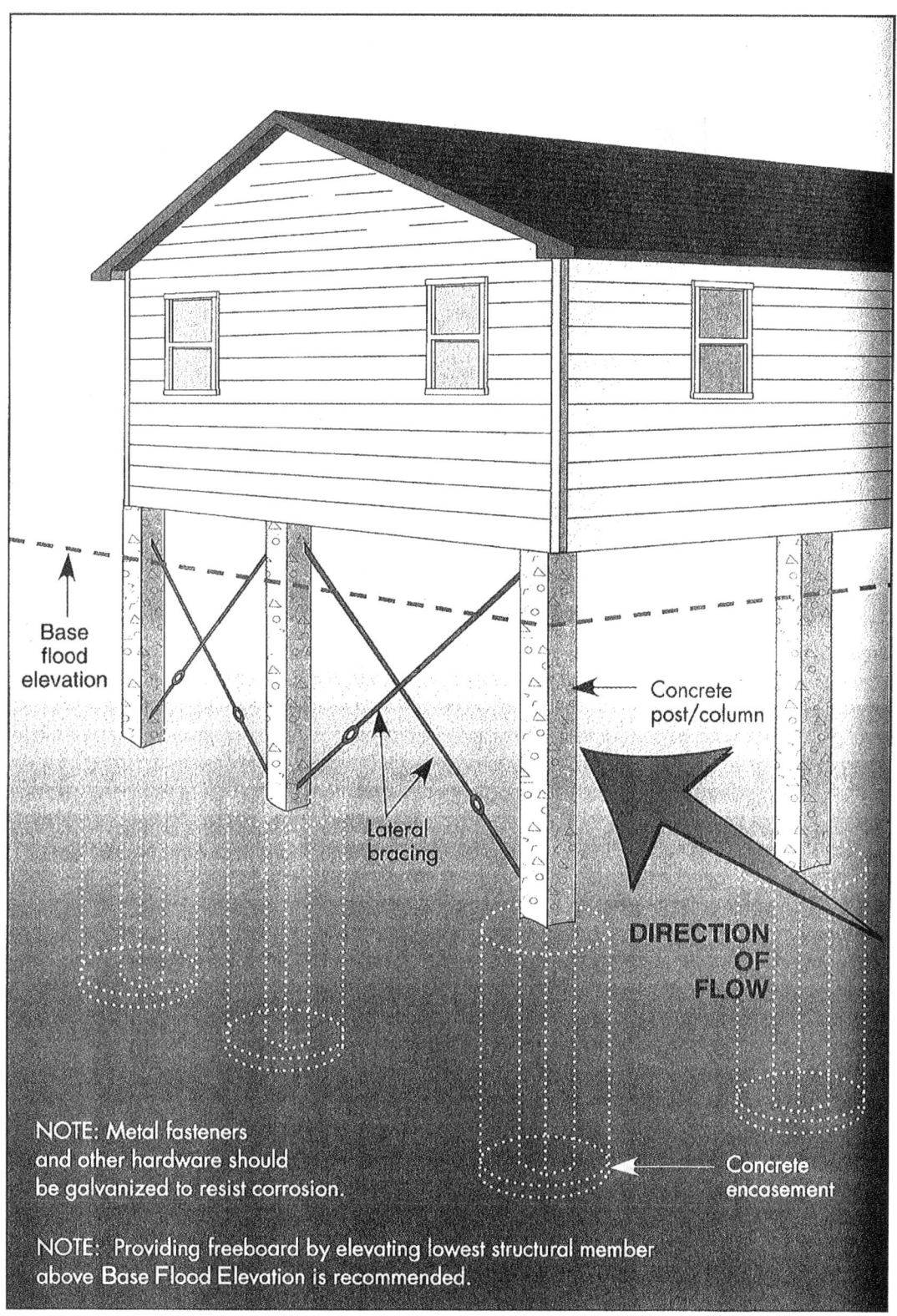

Figure 3-3   Posts can also be anchored in concrete encasements. Where possible, lateral bracing should be oriented parallel to the anticipated flow path (FEMA 1993a).

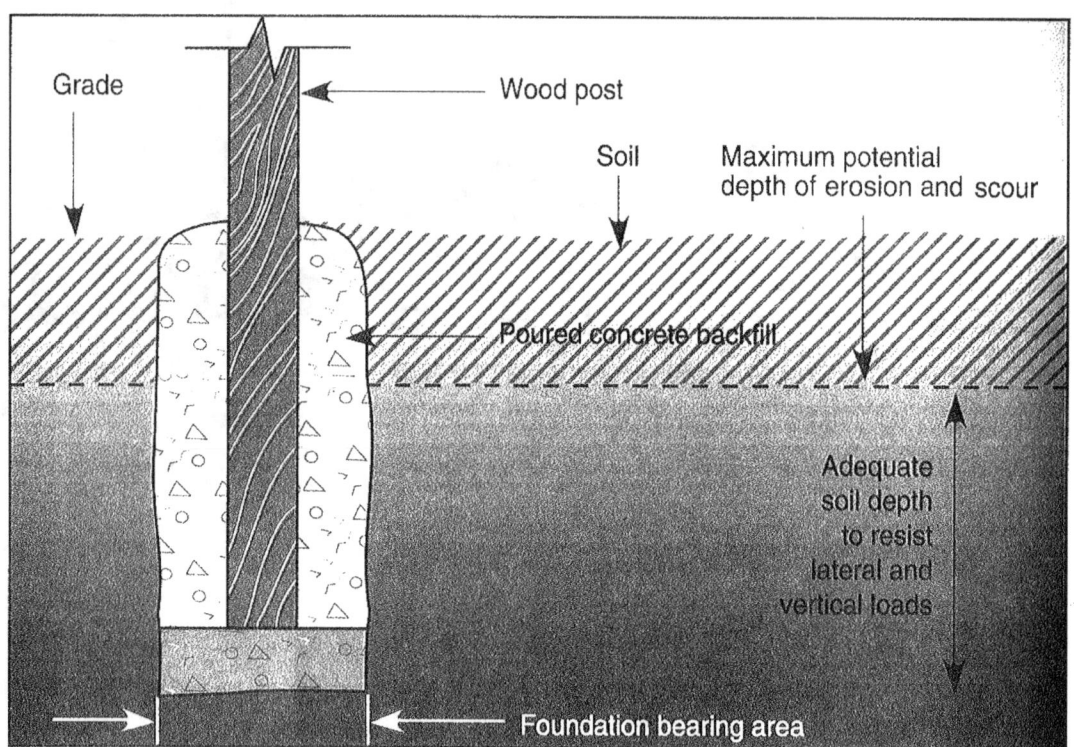

Figure 3-4   Post on concrete bearing pad. Soil depth below maximum potential depth of scour is adequate to withstand lateral and vertical loads during the base flood (after FEMA 1993a).

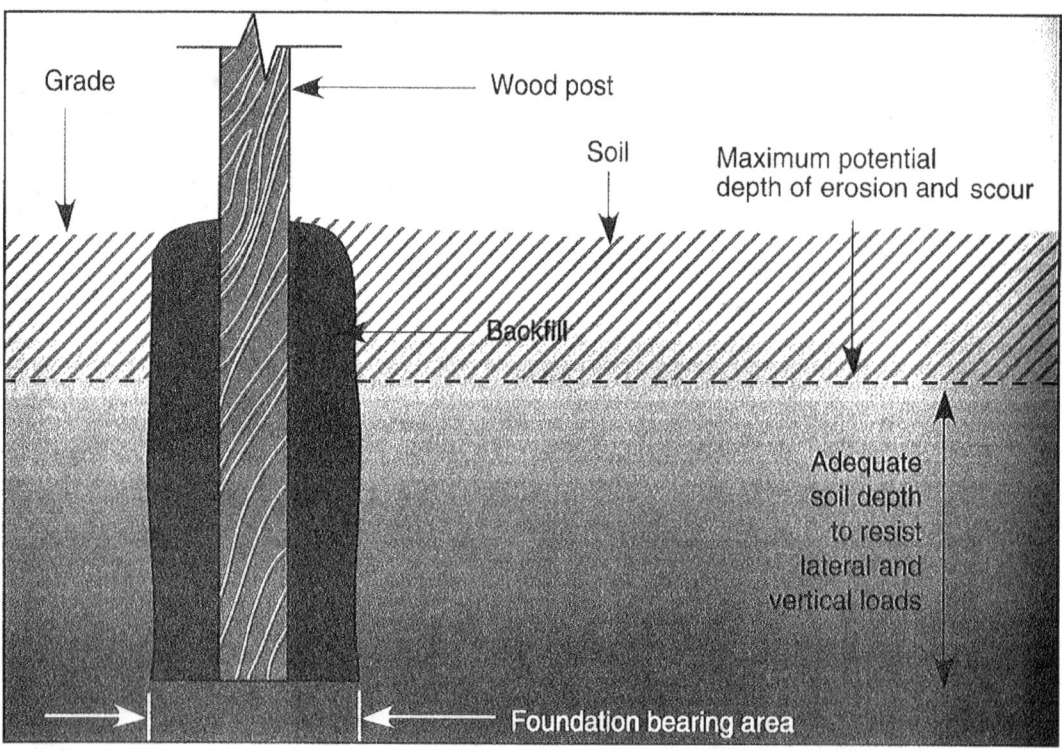

Figure 3-5   Post on earth bearing. Soil depth below maximum potential depth of scour is adequate to withstand lateral and vertical loads during the base flood (after FEMA 1993a).

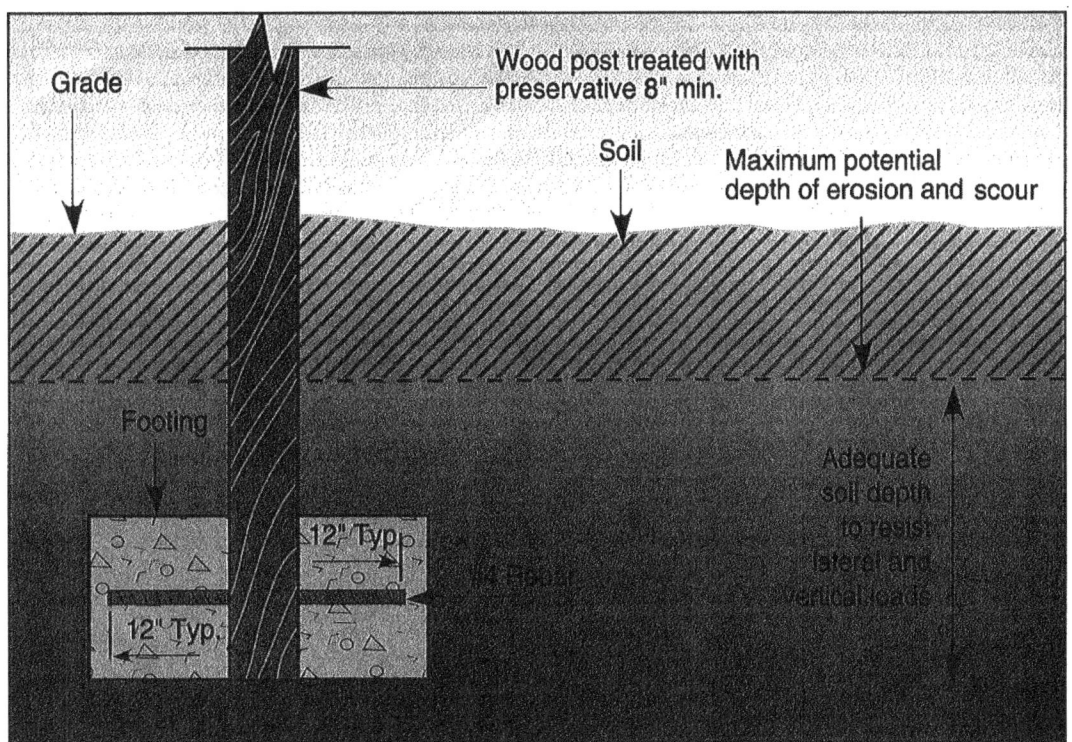

Figure 3-6   *Anchorage of post. Soil depth below maximum potential depth of scour is adequate to withstand lateral and vertical loads during the base flood (after FEMA 1993a).*

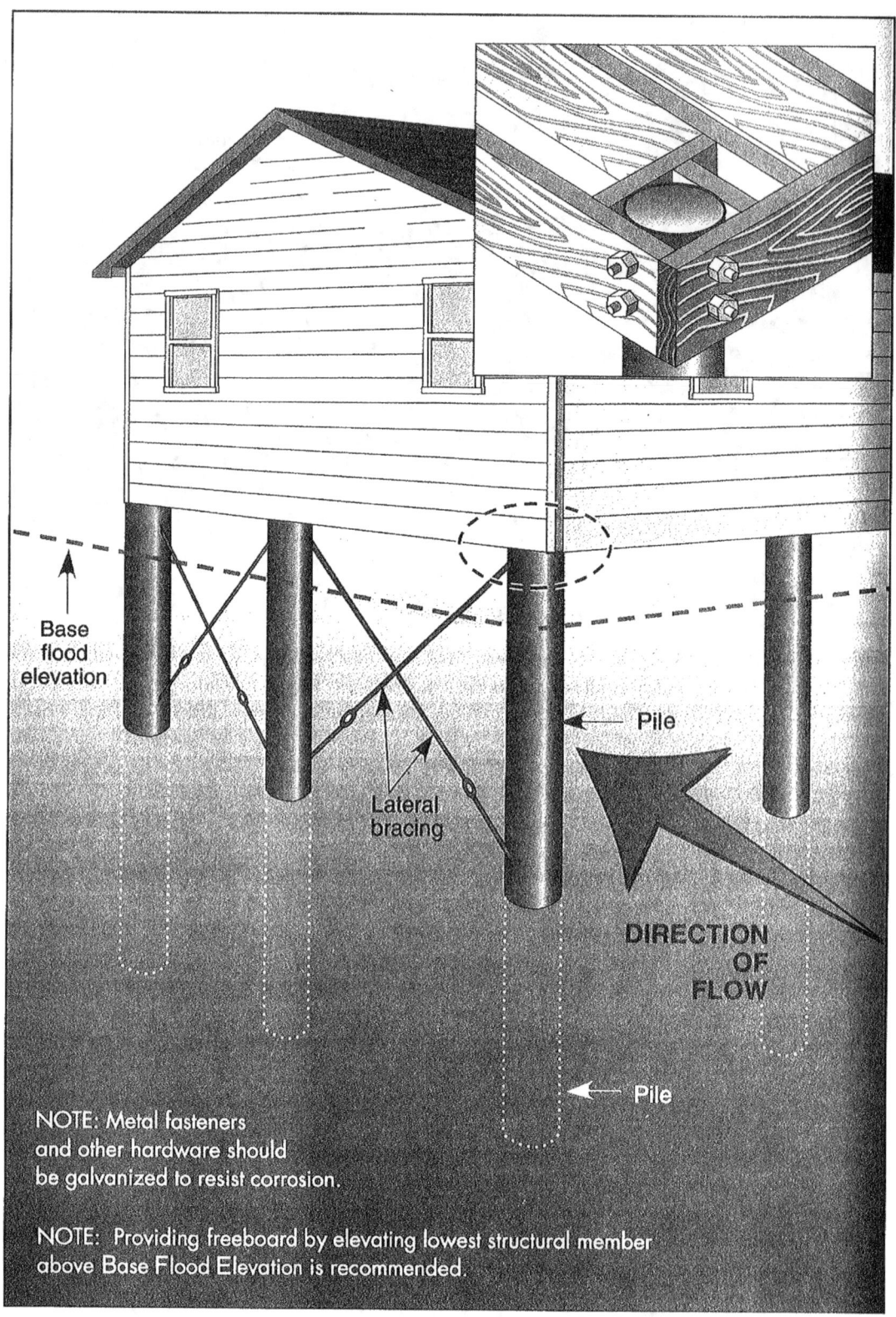

Base
flood
elevation

Lateral
bracing

←— Pile

DIRECTION
OF
FLOW

←— Pile

NOTE: Metal fasteners
and other hardware should
be galvanized to resist corrosion.

NOTE: Providing freeboard by elevating lowest structural member
above Base Flood Elevation is recommended.

Figure 3-7   Piles are mechanically driven into the ground and are therefore less susceptible to high-
velocity flooding, erosion, conical scour, and pullout. Where possible, lateral bracing should
be oriented parallel to the anticipated flow path (FEMA 1993a).

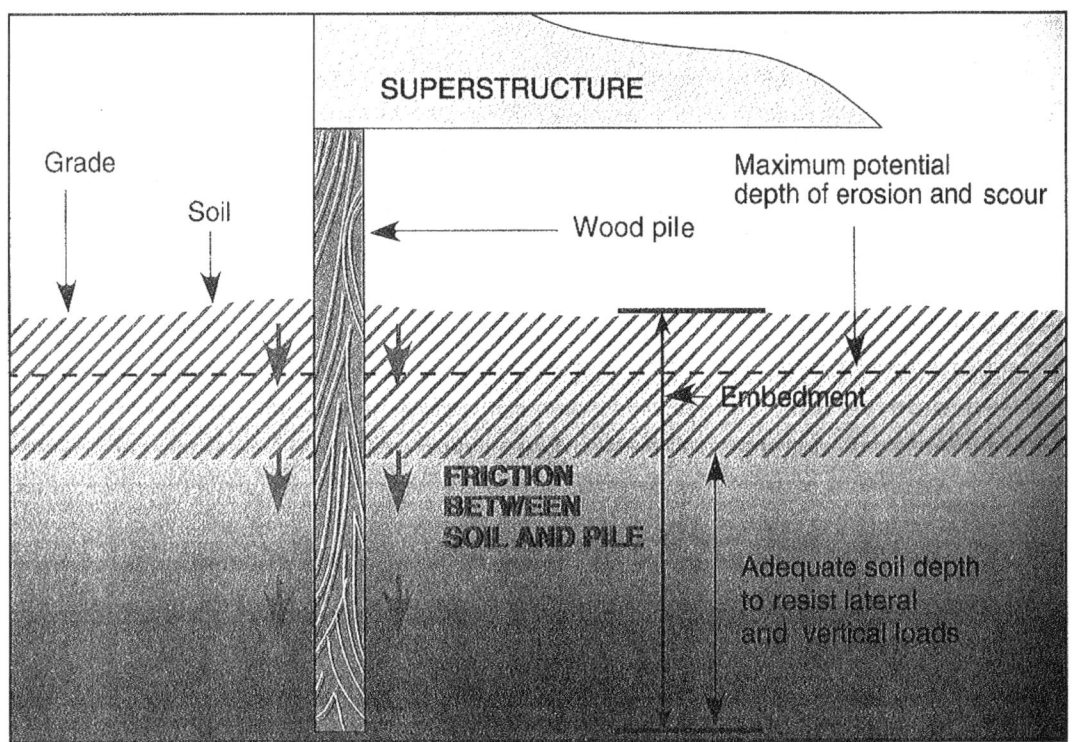

Figure 3-8   The depth of pile embedment provides stability by enabling the pile to resist lateral and vertical loads through passive earth pressure. Soil depth below maximum potential depth of scour is adequate to withstand lateral and vertical loads during the base flood (after FEMA 1993a).

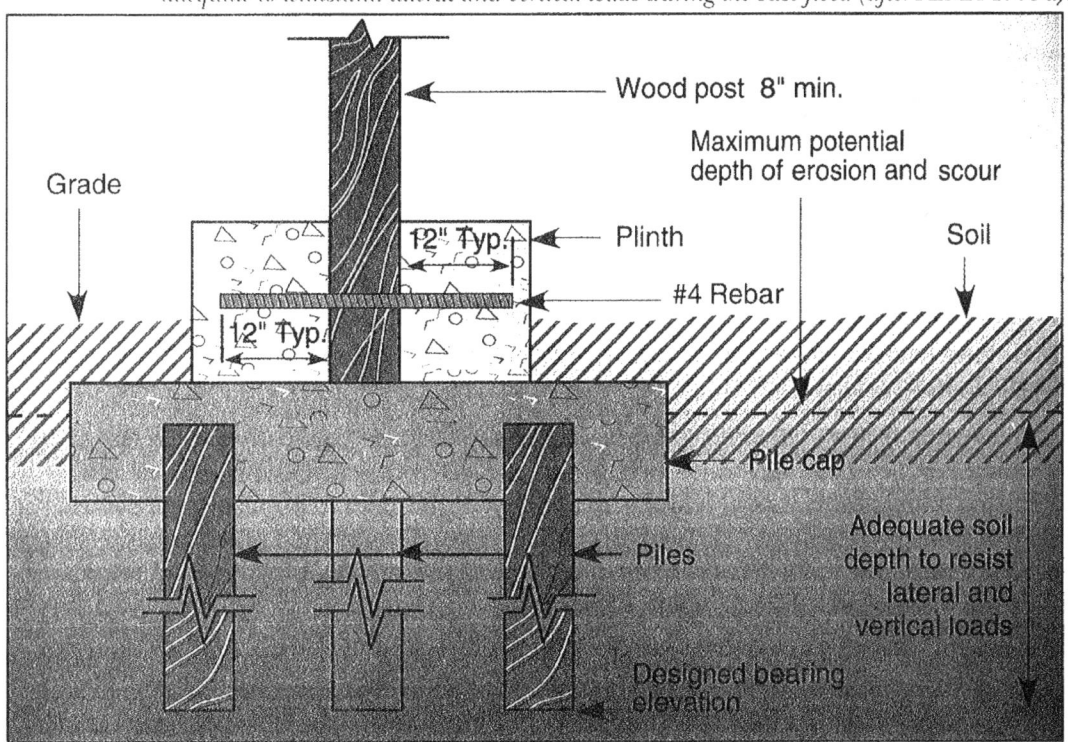

Figure 3-9   Post/pile foundation. Soil depth below maximum potential depth of scour is adequate to withstand lateral and vertical loads during the base flood (after FEMA 1993a).

3.5.3 FRAMING SYSTEMS

Framing systems should be designed to support all anticipated loads, and any cutting of holes for electrical lines, ductwork, or plumbing piping must be in accordance with code requirements. Framing systems should not be compromised by the excessive or improper drilling or cutting of holes. If such drilling or cutting is necessary, additional support may be required to return the structure to its design strength. It is also important that proper bracing and fire stops be included.

3.5.4 CONNECTIONS

All metal connectors should, at a minimum, be constructed of hot-dip galvanized steel and should conform to the Standard Building Code specifications; the guidance provided in FEMA's Technical Bulletin 8-96, *Corrosion Protection for Metal Connectors in Coastal Areas* (FEMA 1996); and any other requirements specified by the design professional of record. Metal connectors include the following:

- wood-to-wood anchors and angles, caps and bases, hangers, and structural connectors

- wood-to-masonry foundation straps, masonry hangers, purlin anchors, plates, tension ties, truss anchors, and brick anchors

- wood-to-concrete anchors and holddowns; bases for beam seats, post bases, and truss seats; hangers; and wedge shims.

Wood should not be used as a shim material since it is subject to compression and may lead to connection failure; instead, metal, brick, or mortar can be used.

3.5.5 BRACING

It is preferable that structures be designed with deep foundations to withstand all anticipated loads without reliance on bracing. However, where used to provide additional stiffening, bracing should consist of hot-dip galvanized steel rods threaded on both ends and joined in the center with a turnbuckle (see Figure 2-10). Alternatively, wood bracing can be used if it is properly designed and attached to piles with bolts. All bracing should be designed as part of the structure by the designer to survive hydrodynamic and debris impact forces generated by the base flood.

3.5.6 BREAKAWAY CONSTRUCTION, FREE-OF-OBSTRUCTION, AND ENCLOSURE REQUIREMENTS UNDER THE NFIP

In general, recently constructed breakaway walls in Coastal High Hazard Areas (V-Zones) and seaward of the CCCL performed well. However, State and local building officials and floodplain administrators should be aware of and should prevent two problems noted during post-Opal damage assessments: (1) breakaway walls attached to walls and other structure elements above the lowest floor and (2) attachment of utility lines and similar components to breakaway walls. In accordance with V-Zone requirements:

- Breakaway walls and panels below an elevated structure must be separate and distinct from walls and construction above the lowest floor elevation. These sections are intended to break free and must be able to do so without damaging upper walls, sheathing, cladding, and other components.

- No wiring, conduits, plumbing, or utility components may be placed behind or fastened to breakaway walls or panels.

- Areas below an elevated building should be designed and constructed in accordance with FEMA's Technical Bulletin 5-93, *Free-Of-Obstruction Requirements for Buildings Located in Coastal High Hazard Areas* (FEMA 1993c).

Figures 3-10 and 3-11 show recommended designs for breakaway wall systems.

3.5.7 STAIRS, DECKS, AND PORCHES

These structures are frequently damaged by floods and storms. Much of this damage can be prevented by the application of a few simple techniques:

- Support elevated decks on piles rather than posts or piers. If a pile foundation is not used for the deck, use knee bracing connected to the foundation piles that support the main structure; however, do not notch the foundation piles to seat the knee bracing.

- Design and construct stairs to hinge at the top, so they can be raised prior to a storm.

- Design and construct fixed steps and walkovers with piles and sturdy structural members. Consider steps and horizontal decks to be sacrificial, and construct them so that they will break loose in small sections when acted on by flood forces.

3.5.8 UTILITIES

All utility components (including electric meters) should be located on the landward side of the structure and, according to NFIP requirements for V-Zones, must be elevated to or above the BFE and anticipated flood level (including wave effects and runup) whenever possible. In A-Zones, utilities may be below the BFE provided that the CCCL requirements are also adhered to. Utility components below the BFE should be contained in floodproof enclosures. Figures 3-12 and 3-13 show recommended designs for mechanical platforms

3.5.9 SEAWALLS AND EROSION CONTROL STRUCTURES

Although permitted in many states and jurisdictions, seawalls, bulkheads, and other erosion control structures should not be relied on to contain soil required for support of a habitable structure. The structure should be supported on a foundation that can withstand or accommodate erosion and loss of support.

Where used, seawalls, bulkheads, and erosion control devices should be designed to resist failure due to wave and flood forces, overtopping, undermining, and debris impact. Wing walls or return walls should extend landward to a point beyond that affected by storm-induced erosion.

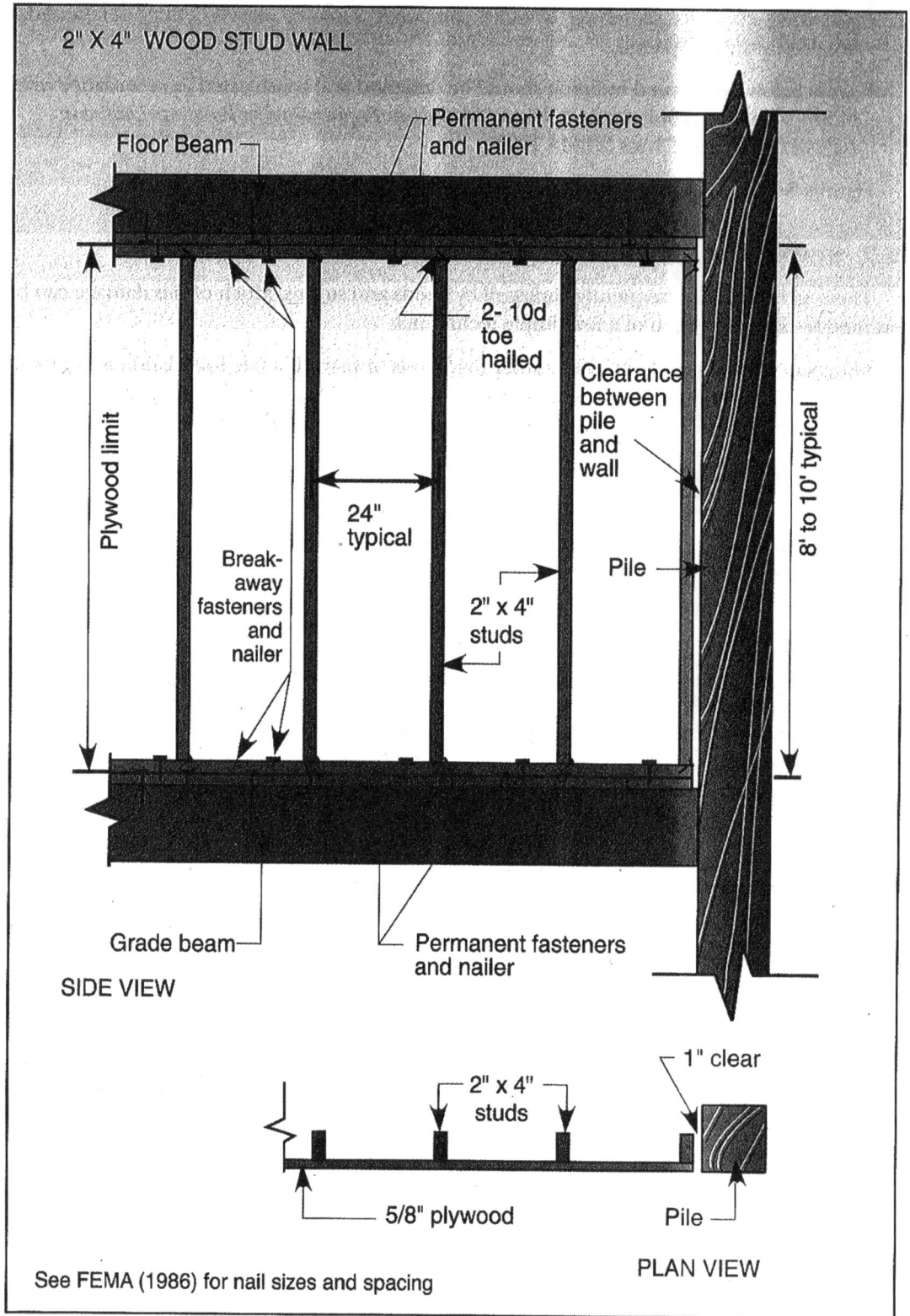

Figure 3-10   Wood stud breakaway wall (after FEMA 1986).

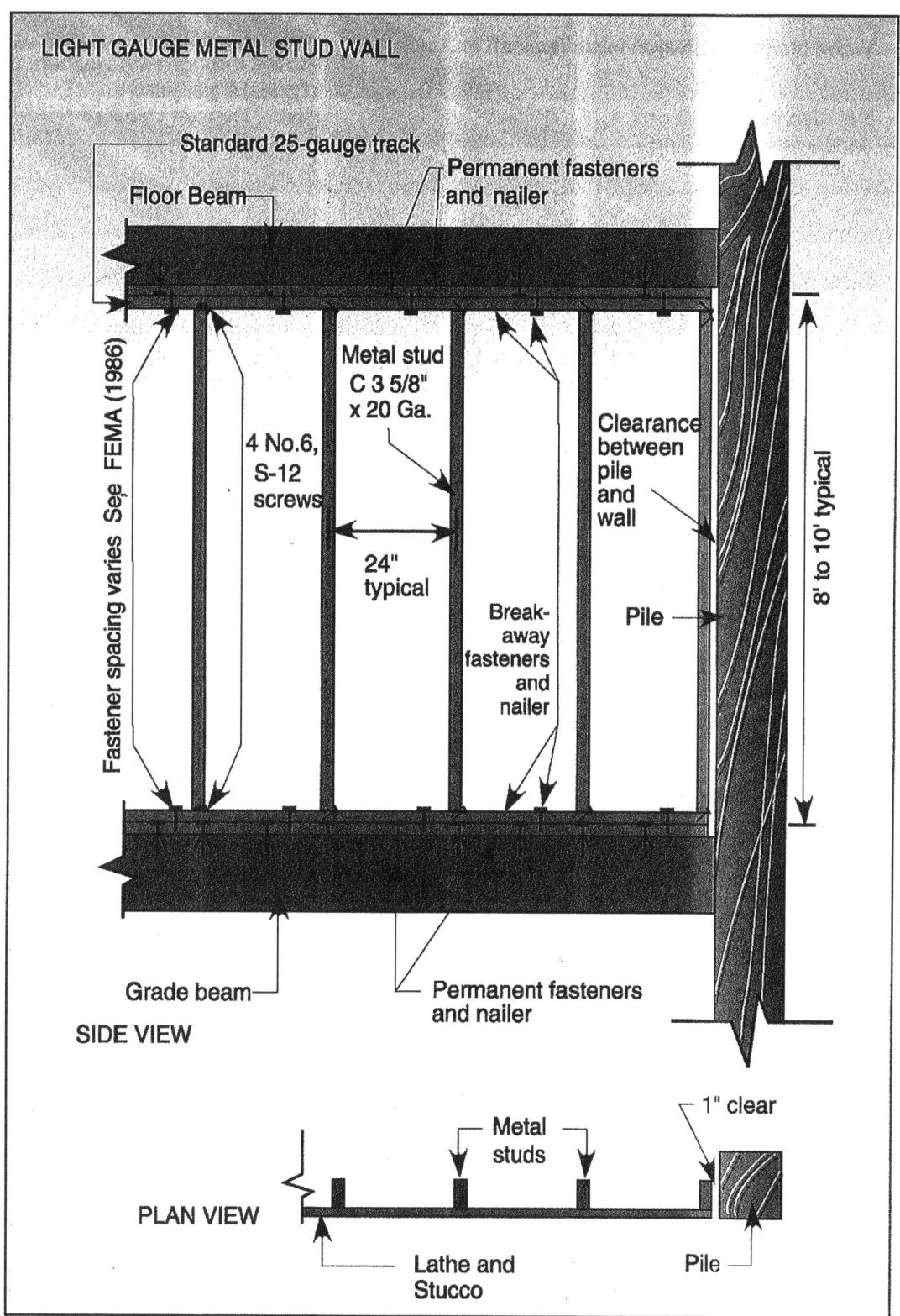

Figure 3-11 Light-gauge metal stud breakaway wall (after FEMA 1986).

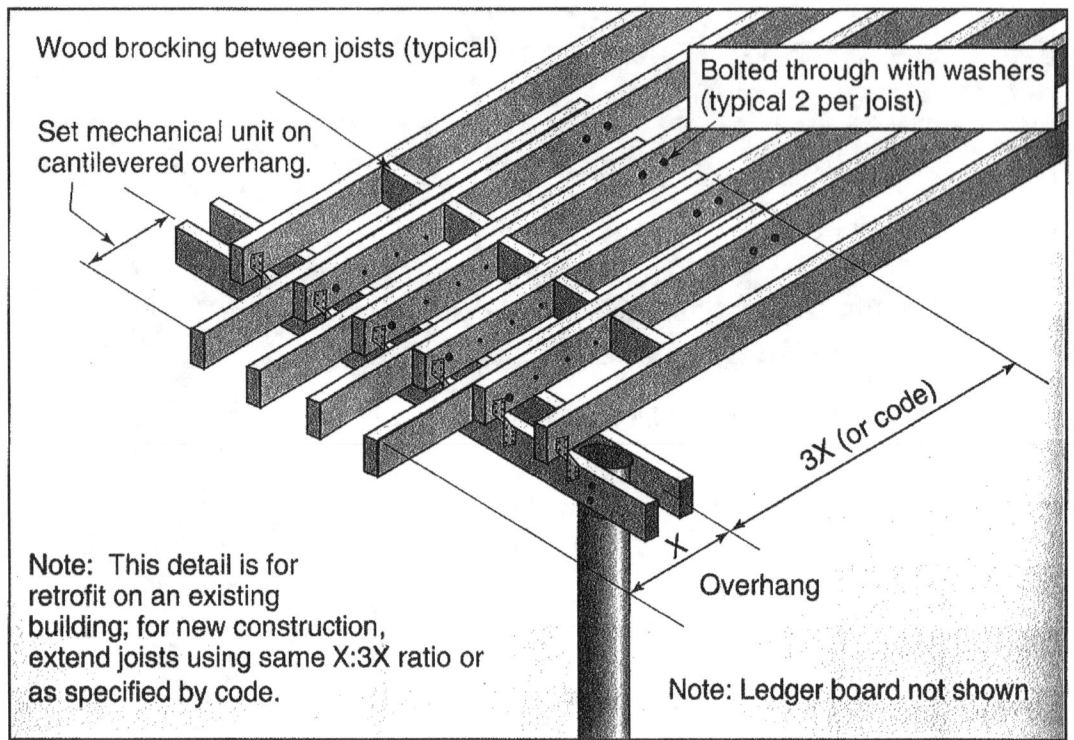

Wood brocking between joists (typical)

Set mechanical unit on cantilevered overhang.

Bolted through with washers (typical 2 per joist)

3X (or code)

X

Overhang

Note: This detail is for retrofit on an existing building; for new construction, extend joists using same X:3X ratio or as specified by code.

Note: Ledger board not shown

Figure 3-12   Installation of cantilevered floor joists as a retrofit for an elevated home to allow for a mechanical balcony.

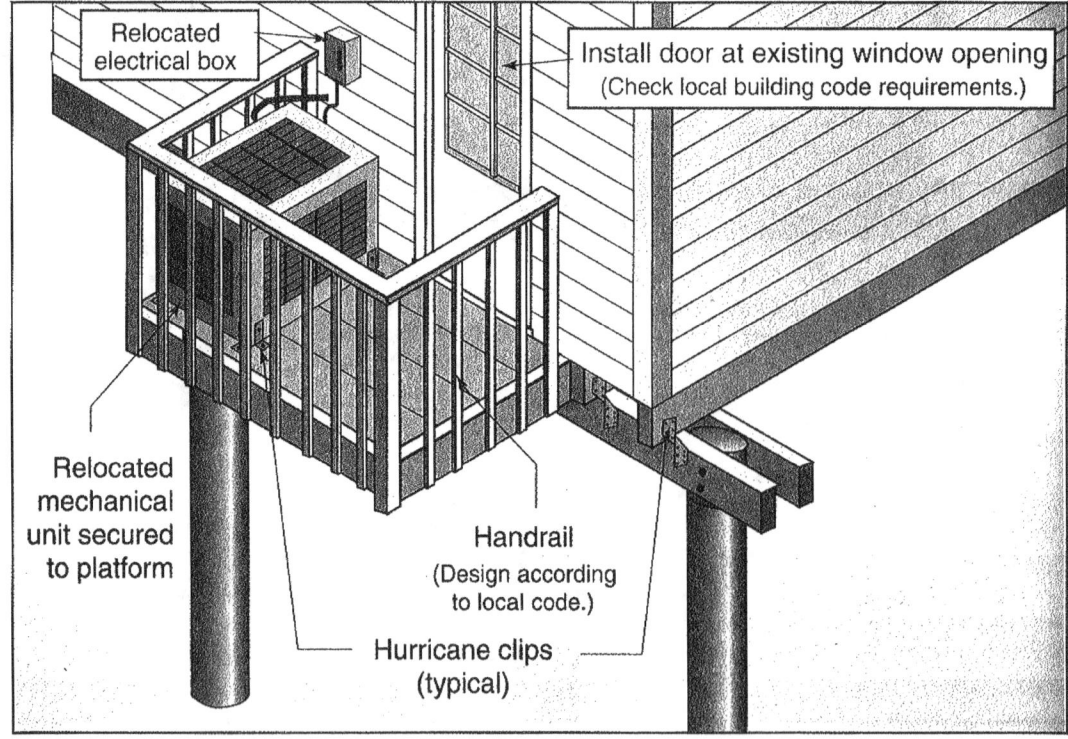

Relocated electrical box

Install door at existing window opening (Check local building code requirements.)

Relocated mechanical unit secured to platform

Handrail
(Design according to local code.)

Hurricane clips (typical)

Figure 3-13   Installation of a mechanical balcony as a retrofit for an elevated home.

4 References

American Society of Civil Engineers, 1995. *ASCE 7-95, Minimum Design Loads for Buildings and Other Structures*. Washington, DC.

Federal Emergency Management Agency, 1986. *Coastal Construction Manual*, FEMA-55. February 1986.

Federal Emergency Management Agency, 1992. *Building Performance: Hurricane Andrew in Florida — Observations, Recommendations, and Technical Guidance*, FIA-22. Federal Insurance Administration. Washington, DC. December 21, 1992.

Federal Emergency Management Agency, 1993a. *Building Performance: Hurricane Iniki in Hawaii - Observations, Recommendations, and Technical Guidance*, FIA-23. Federal Insurance Administration. Washington, DC. January 29, 1993.

Federal Emergency Management Agency, 1993b. *Flood-Resistant Materials Requirements for Buildings Located in Special Flood Hazard Areas*, Technical Bulletin 2-93. Washington, DC.

Federal Emergency Management Agency, 1993c. *Free-Of-Obstruction Requirements for Buildings Located in Coastal High Hazard Areas*, Technical Bulletin 5-93. Washington, DC.

Federal Emergency Management Agency, 1996. *Corrosion Protection for Metal Connectors in Coastal Areas*, Technical Bulletin 8-96. Washington, DC.

Florida Department of Community Affairs, 1995. *Retrofitting and Flood Mitigation in Florida*. Division of Emergency Management. Tallahassee, FL.

Florida Department of Environmental Protection, 1995. *Hurricane Opal: Executive Summary of a Report on Structural Damage and Beach and Dune Erosion Along the Panhandle Coast of Florida*. Bureau of Beaches and Coastal Systems. Tallahassee, FL.

Michael Baker Jr., Inc., 1995. *Hurricane Opal Florida Panhandle Wind and Water Line Survey*. Prepared for the Federal Emergency Management Agency and Property Loss Research Bureau. October 1995.

National Oceanic and Atmospheric Administration, 1995. *Hurricane Opal, Preliminary Best Track and Maximum Sustained 1-min Surface Winds*. AOML, Hurricane Research Division. Miami, FL.

Panama City News Herald, 1995. "Estimated Insured Losses from Hurricane Rises to $1.5 Billion." October 13, 1995, p. 3c.

Appendix

BUILDING PERFORMANCE ASSESSMENT TEAM MEMBERS

MARK A. VIEIRA, P.E.
Civil Engineer
Mitigation Division
Federal Emergency Management Agency, Region IV
Atlanta, GA

TONY SANDIFER
Mitigation Division
Federal Emergency Management Agency, Region IV
Atlanta, GA

DONALD R. BEATON, JR.
Chief Underwriter
Federal Insurance Administration
Federal Emergency Management Agency
Washington, DC

JOSEPH E. PELCZARSKI
Federal Emergency Management Agency, Region I
Boston, MA

SANJAY MANE
Civil Engineer
Florida Department of Community Affairs
Tallahassee, FL

CHARLES R. WEEKS, P.E.
President
The Wainscot Company
Pensacola, FL

J. PAUL HOOFNAGLE
Senior Civil Engineer
Greenhorne & O'Mara, Inc.
Greenbelt, MD

CHRISTOPHER P. JONES, P.E.
Senior Coastal Engineer
Earth Tech, Charlottesville, VA

www.ingramcontent.com/pod-product-compliance
Lightning Source LLC
Chambersburg PA
CBHW080618290526
45790CB00007B/2830